Local Eats
PARIS

A Traveler's Guide

by Natasha McGuinness
illustrated by Anne Bentley

yellow pear press

Library of Congress Cataloging-in-Publication data available
upon request.

Manufactured in Hong Kong.
Design by Rose Wright.

This book has been set in Hypatia Sans Pro.

10 9 8 7 6 5 4 3 2 1

Yellow Pear Press, LLC.
yellowpearpress.com

Distributed by Publishers Group West.

DEDICATION

For my rock star Mama and of

course, Auntie Chris.

Thank you for the free-flowing love,

support, and most

importantly, French wine.

CONTENTS

INTRODUCTION

A mecca of heavenly pastries, flawless dishes, and an abundance of wine and cheese, Paris reigns supreme on my list of top cities for dining. After countless hours of painstaking and rigorous research (kidding—wandering the streets of Paris eating things is one of life's great joys), I have come up with the must-eats of the fabulous French capitol. However, each time I return to Paris, I discover new dishes to fall in love with, fresh local perspectives on cuisine, and slices of artisanal cheese that I would strongly consider shoving a little old lady over, just to get a whiff. Thus, soak up the mouth-watering information presented in this book, but remember—there are always treasures to be unearthed and new finds to be tasted and enjoyed during your time in Paris. It is also important to note that (gasp!) many of the following food items did not originate on the streets of Paris, but are included because they are true favorites of local diners and chefs alike, and have made their mark on Parisian palates.

PÂTISSERIE

Pâtisserie, which is French for both pastry and the shop you buy it in, describes one of the key foods in the Parisian breakfast repertoire. But don't discount these heavenly confections as simply morning treats: they are the perfect pick-me-ups to go with coffee or tea when you need to take a break from feasting your eyes on the scenery and instead feast on the flaky, delicious, sweet, and savory delights found in the many *pâtisseries* nestled into nearly every neighborhood of the city.

CROISSANT

(croissant au beurre v. croissant ordinaire)

At most French *pâtisseries* you will find two different types of *croissants* that are considered to be plain, classic croissants: *croissant au beurre* and *croissant ordinaire*. A common misconception here is that the *croissant au beurre* simply contains more butter than the *croissant ordinaire*. False! The difference is whether or not the croissant is made with butter versus margarine. Most would argue that the *croissant au beurre* is the best way to go, as it features the quintessential taste of Paris: toasted, caramelized, crunchy French butter.

PAIN AU CHOCOLAT

Though directly translated as "chocolate bread," do not be fooled! While chocolate bread may sound good, a chocolate *croissant* (which is what this actually is) is all the better! Traditionally made by wrapping two chunks of dark chocolate in the same layering dough used to make *croissants*, this little treasure is shaped more like a tube or a small loaf of bread. It has the same flaky and airy texture as a plain *croissant*, but is made just a bit more decadent by the addition of the chocolate center.

BEIGNET

Deep-fried dough sprinkled with powdered sugar and occasionally filled with caramel, chocolate, custard cream, or fruit preserves is a regular in Parisian bakeries. Fair warning, however, not all *beignets* are created equal! I've tasted both large and small (think jelly-doughnut size versus chubby doughnut hole) French *beignets* and found that smaller generally means lighter, fluffier, and more moist, as opposed to their larger and drier counterparts. You'll find them either glazed, lightly covered in super-fine sugar, or filled with a variety of jams or creams.

CHAUSSON AUX POMMES

When I first heard about *chausson aux pommes*, I had the following misguided response: "This is just a posh Parisian apple turnover. Ergo: I am unimpressed." Hahaha, no. This is false. *Chausson aux pommes* is all of the good, warm, fussy, happy things in life baked into a flaky pastry. Traditionally, the apple filling is more of an applesauce-like purée as opposed to the chunky American apple pie filling that you might expect. This small change, along with the French's generous use of butter, produces nothing short of perfection.

ORANAIS

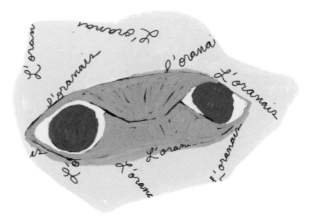

Similar to an apricot *croissant*, this *pâtisserie* favorite is generally made with puff pastry or brioche, and features two large pieces of apricot at each end, as well as a layer of custard and large granules of sugar sprinkled across the top. Somehow, though, it is able to maintain a taste that is not overly sweet, but rather a bit refreshing—for a pastry. It has fruit for goodness' sake. . .just go with it.

MADELEINES

They look like adorable shells and taste like Frenchy heaven, and, oh my goodness, what more could you possibly want? *Madeleines* are small butter cakes, often sprinkled in powdered sugar or half dipped in chocolate, and can be roughly compared to *financiers* in taste. However, *madeleines*, unlike *financiers*, are not made with a browned-butter base, so there is no crispy shell and the sponge texture is less dense.

FINANCIERS

Much like a mini sponge cake, these little rectangular almond cakes are soft, springy, and a great counterpart to an espresso or a cup of afternoon tea. Originating in Paris, these gems are the pride of some of the best Parisian *pâtisseries* as they are seemingly simple, but actually take the skill of a meticulous pastry chef to master. The trick to knowing whether or not you're indulging in a quality *financier*? The edges will be delicately crispy, almost like that of an eggshell, with the inside still retaining its bouncy, spongy texture.

PAIN AUX RAISINS

Flaky *croissant* dough shaped into a shell-like swirl, combined with raisins and a pastry cream filling, makes *pain aux raisins* a cherished breakfast item in France. One of the most tantalizingly delicious aspects of this pastry is the cream filling that allows for a moist inside, while still preserving the ever-pleasing crispy quality of a *croissant* on the outside. The raisins are hydrated beforehand to make them perfectly plump!

PAIN SUISSE

Yet another Parisian favorite, *pain suisse* (translated as "Swiss bread") combines into an elongated shape the same *croissant* dough and pastry cream as many of the aforementioned *pâtisserie* delights, plus loads of chocolate chunks. While similar in taste to the *pain au chocolat*, the *pain suisse* distinguishes itself with the naughty combination of chocolate chunks *and* a cream filling, all while managing to disguise itself as an appropriate breakfast food. But let's be real, you are basically just tricking everyone and eating dessert with your morning *café crème*.

KOUIGN AMANN

Pronouned almost like "queen a-man" with a soft "a" sound, this incredible round pastry somewhat resembles the puffy fabric top of a crown. It is made with layer upon layer of thin dough, as are many Parisian pastries, and has a similar taste to a *croissant*, but the key difference is that it's slightly crunchier. Here's the little secret: while the dough is painstakingly layered, it's sprinkled with sugar in between, creating soft, sweet pockets in the center and a crisp coating on the exterior. *C'est fantastique!*

BOULANGERIE

If you follow the heavenly scent of fresh-baked bread, you'll undoubtedly find yourself in front of the neighborhood *boulangerie,* or bread bakery, where you will discover world-famous *baguettes, croissants,* and other freshly baked French breads piled up and ready for the taking. Absolutely teeming with every bready concoction imaginable and then some, the *boulangerie* is your go-to place for the perfect crusty, puffy, chewy, and flaky taste of France one can conceive of. You can eat them in or take your treats *á emporter*: to go.

QUICHE LORRAINE

While there are many different variations of *quiche*, one of the most popular is *quiche Lorraine*, which originated in the Lorraine region of France and clearly was named by very creative people. This savory pastry is made on an open-faced tart crust and traditionally features light and fluffy eggs, cheese, meat (usually ham) and vegetables (usually onion), and can be enjoyed either hot or cold. It's quite universal since it can be eaten for just about any meal—or even as an indulgent snack!

BAGUETTE

When in Paris, you will likely walk into a *boulangerie* and will find yourself faced with the most difficult decision of your trip: *baguette á l'ancienne* or *baguette traditionnelle*? *Baguette á l'ancienne* costs a little more than a *baguette traditionnelle*, but is handmade slowly from a wild yeast starter, which results in a higher quality artisanal product that will likely meet your dreamy expectations. *Baguette traditionnelle*, while still delicious, is made with the help of machines and may not be up to snuff when compared to handmade *baguette*. My advice is to spend the extra euro and end up with a *baguette* that is exceptional, not just tasty.

BRIOCHE

This soft and supple bun is beautifully simple and flawlessly light and buttery. A *brioche* is a relatively small, distinctly shaped roll and is a staple in Parisian *boulangeries*. It can be eaten on its own (which is particularly delightful since it is slightly sweet), or as a side for both sweet and savory meals. A few exceptionally agreeable pairings include a *brioche* with jam, Nutella, or *foie gras*.

PAIN AUX FIGUES

While most bread traditionally has savory notes, *pain aux figues*, meaning "fig bread," combines bread's naturally savory taste with the sweetness of figs to result in a wonderful marriage of flavors. Available at most neighborhood *boulangeries*, this bread can be found in both larger loaves for you and your *ami*, and smaller loaves for personal eating (the best choice for those of us who are not so great at sharing).

PAIN AUX NOIX

Directly translated as "bread with nuts," *pain aux noix* is a simple and timeless staple in most all Parisian *boulangeries* because of its versatility. Most often baked using walnuts and whole grains, this bread is delicious served plain or toasted and is usually cut into thin slices. Some of the most common cheese pairings tend to be spreadable cheeses such as *chèvre* (goat cheese), *Brie*, or *Camembert*.

PAIN COMPLET

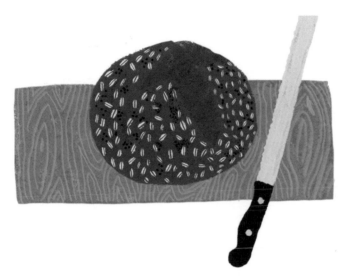

Also known as brown bread, *pain complet* is made from half white bread flour and half whole wheat flour—not to be confused with *pain intégral*, which is made completely with whole wheat flour. This healthy(ish) bread typically takes the form of a loaf, as opposed to the long and skinny *baguette* shape. Since you've clearly made a semi-responsible bread choice, my personal recommendation is that you load up this baby with rich cheese and a hefty portion of *charcuterie* as a reward.

PAIN DE CAMPAGNE

Also called country bread or French sourdough, *pain de campagne* has a rich history and is still celebrated in today's French bakeries. For a large part of France's past, villages have had big communal bread ovens where townspeople brought their dough to bake, to feed their families for multiple days. Today, while usually baked onsite in *boulangeries*, *pain de campagne* most often takes the same traditional, wide-loaf shape that it has long since. It is chewy inside with a satisfyingly thick crust.

PAIN DE SEIGLE

This rustic bread is made with rye and can range in color from light to dark. It is also more dense and chewy than breads made from wheat flour, which makes it perfect to pair with cheese. Stop by a *fromagerie* and enjoy this afternoon snack in one of Paris's many parks. Be sure to bring utensils though, because try as you might, it's nearly impossible to entice park restaurants into lending you cutlery—trust me, I put forth my best, most charming effort to no avail.

BISTRO

Bistro food is usually simple, delicious, home-cooked fare that can be compared to what we think of as diner food, only better. This is where you'll find the classic French dishes that won't disappoint. In need of some French onion soup, bubbling with aromatic cheese and crusty chunks of *baguette*? Look no further. If you're having a hankering for a hearty steak and perfectly salted fries, head to the nearest *bistro*. And if you're feeling more adventurous and would like to try a plate of snails or frogs' legs to round out your Parisian adventure, you'll most likely find them on the menu, too. Most *bistros* have both indoor and outdoor seating with lots of windows that offer wonderful views of the neighborhood and people watching.

LE RUSTIQUE CAMEMBERT

I don't think I have ever come across an order of *le rustique Camembert* that I didn't have a deep and abiding connection with. Considered to be an appetizer and perfect for sharing, this plate of fresh bread laid out to be dipped in the hot, melted, gooey goodness that is *Camembert* cheese straight from the oven is what French lifestyle dreams are made of. Picture a relatively rustic version of fondue, and you've just caught a glimpse of this delicious Parisian culinary adventure.

BLANQUETTE DE VEAU

Translated as "veal in cream sauce," this rich and succulent stew is a cozy way to end a chilly day wandering the streets of Paris. The veal is artfully prepared using a method known as cooking *en blanquette*. Unlike traditionally cooked stews, this dish is made without first browning the meat and fat and made braising a classic method of bourgeois cooking.

SALADE CHÈVRE CHAUD

I wish I could get on a plane right this second and fly back to Paris just for a single bite of this magnificent little number. Directly translated as "hot *chèvre* salad," this simple compilation of ingredients includes small rounds of golden, bubbly *chèvre* cheese atop toasted slices of French bread, nestled among mixed greens, with an olive oil or vinegar-based dressing. You may be thinking, "But it's so simple. What's special about this meager salad?" You'll see when you try it.

STEAK FRITES

Originally made popular through the use of inexpensive cuts of meat made delicious after some serious prep by perfect French chef hands, *steak frites* has evolved into a menu icon. Considered by many to be the national dish of France, this duo of steak and French fries is a simple but timeless menu item that is available at most Parisian *bistros*.

CONFIT DE CANARD

While there are certainly wide ranges in quality for every dish, *confit de canard* (which means duck "cooked in its own fat," making the meat incredibly moist and succulent) is one of those meals where it makes a difference to splurge when choosing a restaurant. Your meal will most likely be delicious regardless of your *bistro* choice, but since *confit de canard* is considered to be one of the finest of the French dishes, when ordered at an upscale establishment, it is usually nothing short of divine. The longstanding traditional French dish is certainly not one to miss during your time in the City of Lights.

SOLE MEUNIÈRE

Craving a little bit of familiarity? Try ordering *sole meunière*, which is a simple and mild fried fish. Sole fillets are dredged in flour, pan-fried in butter, and accompanied by parsley and lemon. It's light and delicious and your taste buds will be hard pressed to forget the delicate flavor. Have a long day of Parisian exploration? This homey dish will restore you, and pairs magnificently with a glass (or two) of white wine.

CUISSES DE GRENOUILLES

If you can get over the fact that these little morsels look exactly like what they are—frogs' legs—you will taste the delicate blend of delicious, tender white meat that's been steeped in the traditional combination of white wine, capers, shallots, and butter, and you'll be thrilled with your order. Humorous side note: the convention of eating frogs' legs can be attributed to a time when French monks were believed to be overeating and gaining too much weight. As a result, the Church banned them from eating meat on certain days, which was impressively thwarted by the monks' ability to have frogs' legs considered a type of fish, thus creating a dish that has become a much loved national delicacy.

SALADE NICOISE

Originally brought together in Nice, in the Provence region of France, *salad Nicoise* is a gorgeous combination of leafy greens, rich oil-cured tuna, perfectly boiled egg, anchovies, small black olives, tomatoes, and may also include a hearty addition of radishes, cucumber, green beans, fava beans, and artichokes. It has everything your body needs to fuel all the walking you'll do while seeing the glorious Parisian sights.

COQUILLES SAINT-JACQUES

One may be surprised to learn that *coquilles Saint-Jacques* is actually a long-celebrated French dish of large sea scallops, which is difficult to gather from the name alone. The scallops are traditionally poached in white wine and served in a beautiful shell filled with a rich mushroom puree, but you may also find this dish as a gratin. Either way, this timeless order is a classic for a reason and will likely never fall from favor with true Parisians.

MOULES

Commonplace in most Parisian *bistros*, *moules*, which are mussels, have long been enjoyed by chefs and diners alike. Traditionally mussels are steamed in a mixture of white wine, butter, and cream, with a blend of ingredients including parsley, garlic, and shallots. Be sure to order a *baguette*—or two—to soak up all the succulent, aromatic white wine juices.

SOUFFLÉ AU FROMAGE

Known to our English-speaking friends as cheese *soufflé*, this savory puff of magic is a must-try during your stay *à Paris*. Egg whites, whipped into stiff, airy perfection, are incorporated into a flour and egg yolk mixture, then gently folded with *Comté* and Parmesan (if the cheese *soufflé* is of the traditional sort) to create something that is mouthwateringly sublime. Try pairing your *soufflé* with a crisp glass of white wine, and *voilá*, you'll be starring in your own French film (with subtitles, of course).

ESCARGOTS

The adage that anything tastes good with enough butter and garlic is put to the test with *escargots*, known to us as snails. After having now dined on *escargot* several times, I have to agree that it is true, because they're delicious—especially when eaten with a *baguette* dipped in the buttery sauce. I can safely say that if you like oysters, mussels, or clams, there is a good chance that you'll also enjoy *escargots*. If you find it more palatable, think of them as "land mussels." The taste and texture are similar. On a separate note, I haven't been able to look my resident garden snails in the eye since my return from Paris.

CROQUE MONSIEUR
CROQUE MADAME

The *croque monsieur* sandwiches thinly sliced ham (known to the French as *jambon*) between toasted, sliced bread that's been coated with béchamel sauce and some Dijon mustard. The sandwich is then sprinkled with *Comté* or *Gruyère*, which decadently melts while the sandwich is being heated on a grill. The *croque madame* is more complex than her male companion (are you surprised?) because in addition to all of the aforementioned goodness, there is an over-easy egg on top, making for a more texturally complex bite.

SOUPE À L'OIGNON

This revitalizing, rich broth is filled with sautéed onions, *baguette* croutons done to perfection, and topped with shredded *Gruyère* or *Comté*—all of which is then baked in the oven until toasty brown. It is the very definition of the whole being worth more than the sum of its parts. The true flavor of Paris, French onion soup is just what's needed to warm up on cold, gray days and is somehow exactly perfect in autumn, spring, and summer as well. It's a classic for a reason.

POT-AU-FEU

Feeling a little homesick while you're abroad? *Pot-au-feu*, translated as "pot on the fire," is a one-pot dish known as the quintessential home-cooked meal served around a French dinner table, regardless of social class or means. Loaded with beef and a feast of vegetables combined in a pot and cooked for hours, *pot-au-feu* allows the slightly tougher cuts of meat to become tender and infuses the savory broth with the rich flavor of the vegetables.

COQ AU VIN

The French seem to have mastered the art of mixing wine and meat, as evidenced in yet another stroke of culinary brilliance. *Coq au vin*, chicken cooked in wine sauce, is fairly similar in concept to *boeuf Bourguignon*. Originally a peasant dish like its compatriot, *coq au vin* was first conceptualized as a way to soften up the meat of roosters; however, modern renditions of *coq au vin* tend to shy away from this and call for hens instead. The braising of this chicken with red wine, *lardons* (a small amount of pork fat), mushrooms, and sometimes garlic makes for a rustic dish that was a treasured favorite of Julia Child.

CASSOULET

Another glorious dish for which we can thank the French peasant-folk, *cassoulet* is a slow-cooked casserole that was first divined as a way to combine leftover ingredients into one cohesive meal. *Cassoulet* is hearty and meant to fill up and warm every nook and cranny of your heart and soul. Customarily made with a combination of white beans, sausages, pork, and lamb, a traditional *cassoulet* is likely to also include goose or duck *confit* with bread crumbs, as well as fried pork or duck skins. Leave it to the French to create something wonderful from using a little bit of this and that found in the larder.

BOEUF BOURGUIGNON

This tender beef braised in red wine and stock originated as a peasant dish, but over time it has become a standard in French cuisine and is even a favorite among upscale *haute cuisine* chefs. First conceived of in the Burgundy region, *boeuf Bourguignon* got its name not because it is a classic Burgundian dish, but because it embodies classic Burgundian flavors: specifically, red wine sauce with mushrooms and small onions.

ENTRECÔTE MARCHAND DE VIN

Two words—meat and wine. Does it get any better? The answer is "No," in case you were wondering. A timeless plate on a French menu, *entrecôte marchand de vin* is exactly that: fried steak drenched in an irresistible red wine sauce that is reduced down after deglazing the pan, resulting in complex layers of flavor that enhance the delicious essence of the meat.

ALIGOT

If there were a magical way that calories didn't count for anything, I would eat a side of *aligot* every day for the rest of my delightfully unrestricted, calorie-free life. Picture cheese fondue and mashed potatoes mixed into one, and you've just arrived at the masterpiece that is *aligot*. This uniquely French country dish is made from mashed potatoes blended with garlic, butter, cream, and all the melted cheese a chef can get his or her hands on.

ON THE GO
STREET FOOD

Paris offers an abundance of delicious and diverse street foods that are perfect to pick up on the go. You'll find food carts, open-air markets, indoor markets, and walk-up windows, all with an abundance of local treats. You can find street carts selling gourmet cheeses, stands offering a variety of *pâtés* and *foie gras, crêpes* and *galettes, falafel, gyros,* and other Middle-Eastern food, incredible chocolates and sweets, roasting chestnuts in the fall and winter, even fanciful cotton candy stands in many parks and gardens. Fruit and vegetable counters filled with flavorful seasonal goods can be picked up to accompany your daily *baguette* while you visit the City of Lights.

JAMBON-BEURRE

Literally translated as "ham butter," the *jambon-beurre* is an easily available, grab-and-go lunch item that is perfect to take with you when you're en route to see the sights of Paris and don't have a moment to spare. It's the ultimate quick French sandwich, consisting of three easy components: a crispy halved baguette, sweet butter, and thinly sliced ham. It's simple, inexpensive, and weirdly fabulous for just being ham and butter.

JAMBON ET
FROMAGE SANDWICH

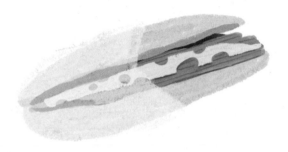

Feeling a little more complex? Try opting for the ever-satisfying *jambon et fromage sandwich*, which serves basically the same purpose as the *jambon-beurre* (see previous swoon-worthy item), but includes *Emmental* cheese instead of butter. Shocking, right? If the sandwich provider of your choosing is feeling particularly fancy, they may include some mixed greens or small French pickles for a little added pizazz.

CRÊPES & GALETTES

With *crêpes* and *galettes* being the pinnacle of quintessential Parisian street food, you'd be hard-pressed to find a Parisian *crêperie* that is not fabulous. *Crêpes* are very thin, large pancakes that are used to wrap endless fillings. *Crêperies* offer a wide array of both sweet and savory *crêpes*, with the sweet *crêpes* usually being made with *crêpe* batter and the savory made with *galette* batter (essentially the same things as a *crêpe* but made with buckwheat and no sweet notes to be found).

SAUCISSON

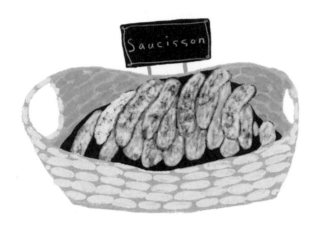

Similar to whole salami or sausages, *saucisson* is a type of thick, dried, cured meat that got its start in France. While *saucisson* typically is made with pork or a mix of pork and other meats, there are an infinite number of meat combinations, all of which boast their own reasons to love them (my personal favorite is duck *saucisson*). You can find this divine meat in street markets or near the *charcuterie* at grocery stores, as well as in *boucheries* (butcher shops). Most all vendors are happy to let you taste a number of their products before you buy, which makes for a fun comparison and an assurance of no buyer's remorse.

FOIE GRAS

While *foie gras* is a controversial food item in the United States, it is a French delicacy and something to be tried if you are so inclined. Specially fattened duck or goose liver, commonly described as rich and buttery, *foie gras* is often enjoyed spread on a delicate cracker or thin slice of freshly baked bread. *Foie gras* is one of the most well-known types of *pâté* (a mixture of ground meat and minced fat blended into a paste). Do note, however, that the process of fattening the ducks and geese brings up some animal-rights concerns, so proceed with caution if this is something that you are sensitive to.

RILLETTES

Similar in concept and preparation to *pâté*, *rillettes* is meat that is cubed and then cooked slowly until it is tender enough to be shredded. It is then mixed with cooking fat and blended into a rustic paste—which can be spread onto toast or crackers. Over the years, *rillettes* has grown in variety and now is deliciously made with most all meats, including fish. The secret to discerning the quality of *rillettes* hides in the consistency of the paste: if it boasts a smooth and soft texture, you know it's been done right.

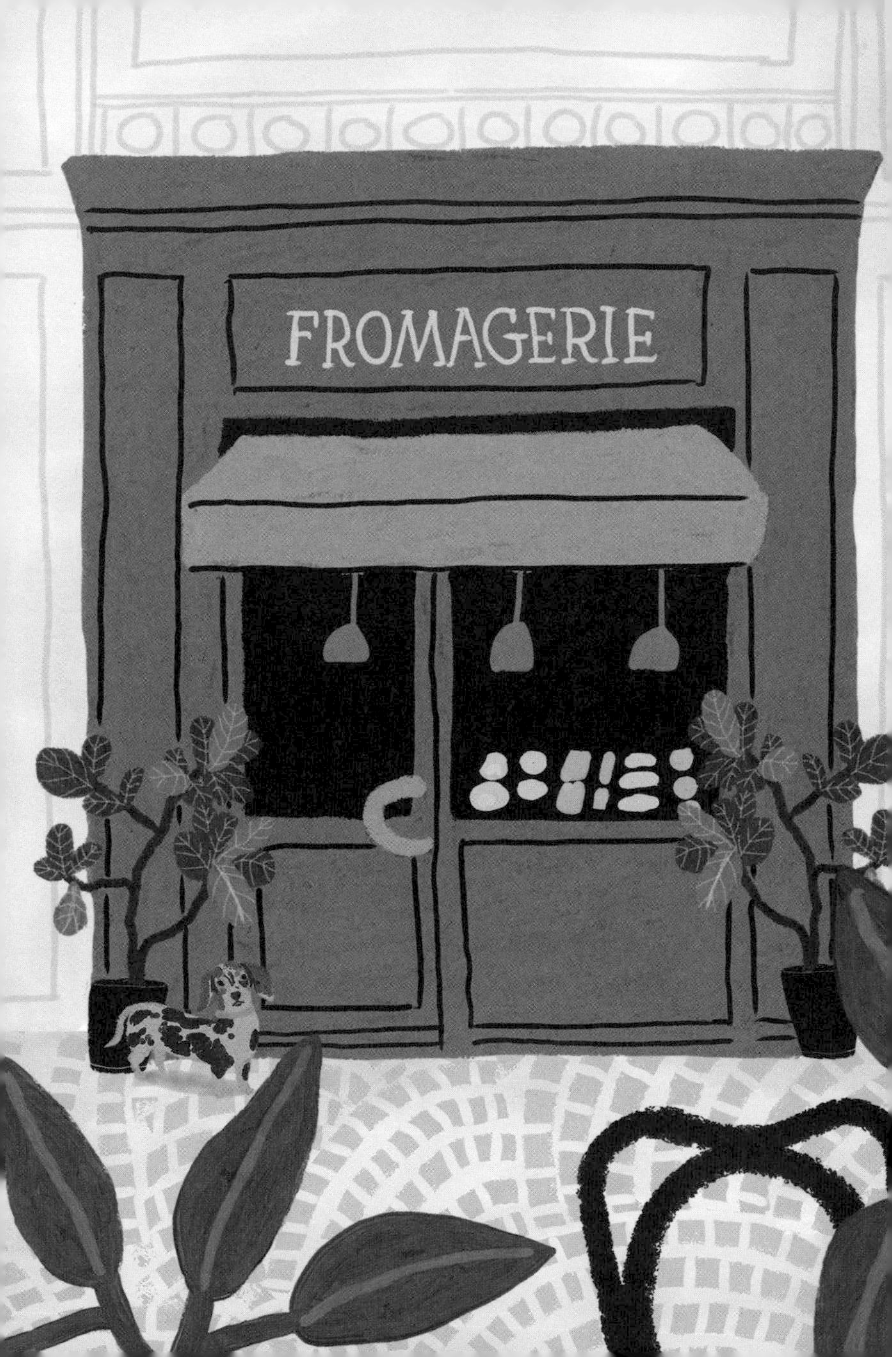
FROMAGERIE

FROMAGERIE

Charles de Gaulle once famously quipped, "How can you govern a country that has 246 varieties of cheese?" And while France now has many more varieties than that, there are three main types of cheese to help identify and classify what's what. They are pressed cheese, soft cheese, and blue cheese. And then, of course, there are different types of milk used within each category, including cow's milk, goat's milk and sheep's milk. The region from which the delectable *fromage* hails is a factor, too. And, oh yeah, cheeses are then further divided depending upon whether they are small batch, artisan farmhouse cheese, or manufactured cheese, so the following is a small primer of French favorites so you don't become completely overwhelmed while standing at the counter of the *fromagerie.*

TOMME DE SAVOIE

Hailing from the French Alps, *Tomme de Savoie* is a traditional cheese that has long been a part of French history. It is made year-round from cow's milk and has a slightly different taste and color depending on whether it is made with milk from cows that have been fed primarily summer grass versus winter hay. It has a relatively low fat content for cheese, is moderately firm, and has a fairly thick rind. In my opinion, this masterpiece of a cheese is best eaten in slices on its own, as it is not overly rich. It's also fabulous accompanied by sliced apples *(pommes)*.

ROQUEFORT

One of the most famous of French blue cheeses, *Roquefort*, can be likened to that friend who talks louder than everyone else, hijacks other people's funny anecdotes, and always wants to be the life of the party. Basically, it has a strong personality and won't let you forget it. It's a type of blue cheese made from sheep's milk—it's semi-hard, crumbly, and straight up delicious if you're in the mood for some pungent cheese.

REBLOCHON

This washed-rind and smear-ripened cheese has a distinct softness and is made with raw cow's milk. Here's what that means: the rind of the cheese is occasionally washed in a briny saltwater and/or liquids that are molding agents, such as beer, wine, brandy, spices, etc. Some washed-rind cheese are also smear-ripened, which is the process of introducing solutions of bacteria or fungi, and gives the cheese a stronger flavor as it continues to mature.

PONT-L'ÉVÊQUE

Pont-l'Évêque is an unpressed and uncooked cow's milk cheese that generally features a washed-rind (see *Reblochon* for details of this process) with a creamy, yellow-colored center. It has a smooth, velvety texture and has been made since at least the twelfth century. So here's your takeaway: this cheese is practically ancient, which means that the French have had centuries to perfect it, ergo it is spectacular.

COMTÉ

This semi-hard, pressed cheese, formerly known as *Gruyère de Comté*, is made from unpasteurized cow's milk and is one of the most beloved and used cheeses in all of France. *Comté* has the highest production rate of all the French cheeses, is aged in gorgeous large rounds in caves (could it get any better?), and has a taste that is fairly strong and slightly sweet. Its ability to melt easily makes it popular for everything from cheese *crêpes* and fondue to *croque monsieur.*

CHÈVRE

Pure glory has been bestowed upon us all in the form of *chèvre* (goat cheese). *Chèvre* can be soft and creamy and perfectly spreadable or a little bit more crumbly depending on how it's made. Often accompanied by herbs, *chèvre* is the quintessential soft French cheese and can be enjoyed on bread, crackers, and even warm in *chèvre* salads.

LIVAROT

One of France's oldest varieties of cheese, *Livarot* has the distinction of having been notably mentioned in literature as far back as 1693. While being aged, the cheese is circled by five bands of rush leaves, which look a bit like the five stripes worn by colonels. As a result, this cheese has the unique fortune of being nicknamed "the colonel." One of the many reasons *Livarot* is a Parisian foodie favorite is because it is easily adapted to accompany a wide range of dishes and can be served both warm or chilled.

CAMEMBERT vs BRIE

Originating from Normandy, *Camembert* is a soft and creamy cheese made from cow's milk and is often compared to *Brie*, which is similar in appearance and is also made with cow's milk. *Brie*, however, is made in Ile-de-France. A few key differences between these two French favorites include size (*Brie* tends to be packaged in larger wedges or moons) and fat content (*Brie* generally has a slightly higher fat content than *Camembert*). But the fact is, if you like soft cheeses, these are both for you.

LES DESSERTS

Les desserts, or simply the dessert course, is not to be missed during your stay in Paris. Whether perfect melt-in-your-mouth *chocolat,* world-famous meringues, salted caramel, airy custard-filled *pâtisseries*, colorful *macarons*, or elegant cakes and tarts, the French are somehow able to take the mixing of sugar, eggs, and butter to another level entirely. In the glorious capital of decadence, you'll be able to find a satisfying sweet to answer the call of your every sugary desire.

GATEAU OPÉRA

Prepare yourselves for complete perfection! Layers of almond sponge cake are first soaked in coffee and then slathered in chocolate *ganache*, coffee buttercream, and finished with a chocolate glaze. This process is done a few times over and results in a delicate cake that's almost too pretty to eat. Almost.

TARTE TATIN

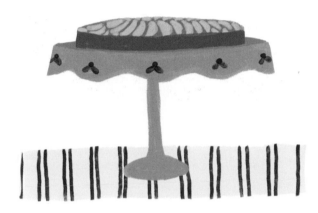

This sweet treat is an upside-down pastry, which includes caramelized fruit (usually apples). The fruit is first lathered in butter and sugar, caramelized, and baked with a crumbly, salty crust—heaven? I think yes. While it is not quite as patriotic as apple pie, it certainly put the perfect French twist on this American classic!

CHOCOLAT

You simply can't experience Parisian cuisine in an authentic and local way without giving some serious love to the chocolate shops that call this city home. French *chocolat* is just as much a mouthwatering indulgence as it is an art form. The endless options of different types of chocolate on display in Parisian *chocolateries* may seem overwhelming, but the truth is that it is nearly impossible to make a wrong choice in this delightful scenario. A few interesting things to note before diving in: *chocolateries* traditionally are both makers of chocolate as well as shops to buy chocolate. Further, the basic shapes of these artisanal delicacies tend to be simple and sleek, as they are made by hand instead of machine-made molds.

ST. HONORE

Named for the patron saint of pastry chefs and bakers, this legendary cake certainly lives up to its heavenly name. The *St. Honore* cake features a base of puff pastry surrounded by a ring of *pâte à choux* (light pastry dough also used to make *beignets*, *éclairs*, *profiteroles*, and basically 80 percent of all other pastries). It is then topped by small cream puffs, which have been dipped in caramelized sugar. Finally, the remaining space is filled in with pastry cream, and the cake is topped with whipped cream, which is piped on using a special frosting tip that is unique to the *St. Honore* cake.

PROFITEROLES & ÉCLAIRES

Also known as cream puffs, *profiteroles* are a no-fuss treat that are a bit more down-to-earth than some of their fellow sweet counterparts. Generally topped with rich chocolate sauce, these hollow rounds of *pâte à choux* can be filled with cream, ice cream, whipped cream, or custard. Much like the *profiterole*, the *éclair* is made with the same dough and cream filling, but is longer and cylindrical in shape. *Éclairs* are also topped with a wide array of icing flavors and *ganache*, as opposed to the more traditional, thinner glaze choices generally drizzled over a *profiterole*.

RELIGIEUSE

Named for the (quite vague) resemblance to a nun's habit, the
religieuse is made of the ever-popular previously discussed
pâte à choux. The bottom round of *pâte à choux* serves as a
base for a smaller round (or two, depending on the bakery)
that makes up this multitiered dessert. All are filled with pastry
cream and drizzled in chocolate or mocha. Feeling whimsical?
Try the *religieuse violette*, which is purple and boasts a soft,
floral violet flavor.

PARIS BREST

If you can manage to not giggle like a tween boy when ordering this magnificent creation, then you're in for quite the extravagant dessert. Also made with *pâte à choux*, found in a number of the aforementioned treats, the *Paris brest* looks much like a doughnut that has been cut horizontally through the middle. Sweet hazelnut and praline cream is then sandwiched in the center, and a light dusting of almond slivers is sprinkled over the top, creating a relatively simple yet refined pastry.

MACARONS

Arguable one of the best inventions ever to happen in a French bakery, *macarons* alone are worth the trip to Paris. These cookies get their light and airy texture from the egg-white base that is used to make them, which also makes *macarons* especially delicate and complex. Though there are seemingly endless flavors and fillings of *macaron*, especially in the *macaron* mecca that is Paris, some of the more traditional flavors include chocolate, pistachio, coffee, and raspberry. But let's be honest—if the *macaron* is made well, the filling is simply secondary.

CANELES

Ah, yes, *caneles*: the official sponsor of all your Parisian dreams. Known for being notoriously fussy and technically tricky to bake, these little bites of perfection are originally from the Bordeaux region of France, but have made their way into the hearts of Parisians all the same. The small, moist, rum-flavored cake has a custardlike center and caramelized coating from being baked inside a flute-shaped tin (like a cupcake pan, but with deeper fluted cups). It makes for the perfect two-bite sweet delight.

MILLE-FEUILLE

The list of ever-magical French desserts continues with this delicate slice of finely layered cake. The *mille-feuille*, which means "a thousand leaves," is made up of three layers of puff pastry with alternating coatings of pastry cream, whipped cream, jam, or custard and is usually finished with an icing top. Note: other English names for this cake include vanilla slice, custard slice, or Napoleon.

BABA AU RUHM

Invented in Paris, the *baba au ruhm* is the definition of a Parisian classic! This little devil is a small yeast cake that is soaked in high-proof liquor (usually rum, *mais oui*) and is often served with a whipped cream or pastry cream. The yeast-based batter makes for a particularly airy cake, which allows it to take on a spongy quality in order to soak up as much alcohol as possible. The end result? An indulgently boozy confection that is served well *flambéed*.

KOUGLOF

Rumored to be brought to France via Alsace by Marie-Antoinette, the *kouglof* (which is a cake—how appropriate!) was a favorite of this infamous royal. Generally enjoyed with breakfast or a cup of afternoon tea, this breadlike bundt cake is moist in texture and made perfectly sweet by the use of nuts, raisins, and sometimes even brandy. Can't find *kouglof* on the menu anywhere? It is often only served on the weekend and is also known as (prepare yourself) *gougelhof, kougelhof, gugelhupf, kugelhof, kugelopf,* or *kugelhopf.*

MONT BLANC

Also known as a chestnut cream cake, the *Mont Blanc* is a chilled dessert made with a puree of sweetened chestnuts that have been piped into the shape of a nest and topped with whipped cream. These petite delights, whose name directly translates as "white mountain," are named for the snowcapped mountains that they resemble!

TARTE AU CITRON

While lemon tarts can be found in many countries, the *tarte au citron* is a longstanding traditional French dessert and can be found in most any Parisian bakery. While many lemon tarts are quite sweet, the *tarte au citron* generally has a more full, sharp citrus flavor and (of course) is baked in a buttery crust that is capable of reducing large burly men to tears.

CRÈME BRULEE

If the word *enchanting* had a taste, it would taste like *crème brulee*. Think I'm overexaggerating? Try this divine custard before you start calling in complaints! Also known as burnt cream, *crème brulee* is a well-known and much loved French classic, which is made up of a rich custard with a hard, caramelized sugar top and is generally served at room temperature. Use the back of your spoon to crack through the amber-colored sugar top and indulge.

CLAFOUTIS

If this gorgeous, baked little number seems like a simple fruit tart, you, my dear culinary friend, are sorely mistaken. *Clafoutis* takes the best components of custard and of a tart and combines them to make a sweet country dessert. Fruit (customarily black cherries) is enveloped in a thick batter that resembles flan and baked in a (you guessed it) buttery crust. This dish is most often served in the summer months and is considered to be a more rustic, casual dessert.

FAR BRETON

Similar to the flanlike base used in *clafoutis* batter, the *far Breton* is originally from the Brittany region of France and is another fan favorite. While flan-y cake with the addition of prunes or raisins may sound like your great grandmother's favorite excuse to get rid of dried fruit, I swear it is in fact quite delicious! After all, classics become classics for a reason, right?

MERINGUES

The combination of whipped egg whites and sugar result in the cloudlike texture of these unique cookies, which are sometimes baked with acidic flavors such as lemon to infuse a light note. While the short ingredient list may fool some into thinking these require little skill to make, the reality is that immense precision and technique are required to make the perfect *meringue*. Because the main ingredient is egg white, these little confections are a great way to go if you're looking for a low-fat dessert.

CARAMEL AU BEURRE SALÉ

Not to be confused with salted caramel, *caramel au beurre salé* is made with salted—instead of unsalted—butter, which results in a more subtle and blended salty flavor than classic caramel that salt has been simply added to. Salted butter caramel can be either made into a sauce to enjoy alongside other treats (or on a spoon if you have little to no self control like me) or made into chewy caramel candies. A few particularly heavenly suggestions include salted butter caramel crêpes or salted butter caramel drizzled over vanilla ice cream.

FOOD ORDERING GUIDE

Here are some words and phrases that will help you order like a native—or at least help you get what you want.

La carte is what a menu is called.

À la carte means "from the menu" when directly translated, but what it actually means is that you will be ordering specific food items, and those food items do not come with extras, such as salad. If you want extras, you have to order them separately.

Plat du jour is the daily special.

Prix fixe is what a menu is called that has one price for the whole shebang. You'll get a full-course meal, often with limited choices, but the price is usually better than if you order each course separately.

Je voudrais, s'il vous plait means "I would like, please."

And let me say that the "please" goes a long way toward being thought a polite person and toward getting what you want. Learn it, use it, love it.

If you would like to get the attention of a member of the wait staff, the way you do that is to say, *S'il vous plait, Monsieur* or *S'il vous plait, Madam* (or *Mademoiselle* if the female in question is a teenager or obviously a young woman). This phrase will get you much farther than a snap of the fingers or a wave.

Here's a handy little phrase to learn if you know what you want on the menu, but you don't want to attempt to speak in French, you can point to the menu item and say, *Ce plat là*, which means "This item (or plate) here."

If you are ordering beef and would like it cooked to a certain doneness, here are the three possibilities: *rosé*, meaning "rare", *à point*, meaning "medium-rare," and *bien cuit*, meaning "well-done."

Un apéretif is a pre-dinner cocktail.

L'entrée This one might throw you off because, unlike in the United States, the entrée is not the main course. It's an appetizer.

Le plat principal This one is pretty self-explanatory. It's the main dish. It's your chicken, fish, beef, pork, or lamb.

Un morceau means "a piece" and is the perfect thing to use when you want to order a piece of just about anything you can think of—except cake, which is ordered by the slice rather than by the piece.

Une tranche means "a slice." This is how you order your cake, bread (other than full loaves or baguettes of course) and meat if it's sliced. There's another word for a slice of fruits or vegetables, so keep that in mind.

Une rondelle This also means "slice" but is used fruits for and vegetables.

Un verre de vin means a glass of wine, which is important to your French experience.

Le dessert You've got it! It's the dessert, or as the British would say, "pudding."

Le fromage Assuming you've now read the chapter about the cheeses of France, you'll surely guess that this is the cheese course. In France, many people eat a cheese course instead of dessert. I know…what's up with that?

Le digestif This is an after-dinner drink that's supposed to promote digestion. Really? Those French!

C'est terminé means "We're done eating."

L'addition s'il vous plaît means you would like the bill please. This is what you can say to signal that you are ready to pay and leave.

At the bottom of some bills, you will see either *Service Compris* or *Service Non Compris*, which means either the tip is included or not included, respectively. If you are unsure, you can also ask. Do note that tipping is very different in France than in the United States, where leaving 15 to 20 percent of the total bill is customary. In France, leaving a few Euros on the table is the way to go.

Bon Appétit!

ACKNOWLEDGEMENTS

An endless outflow of gratitude and sincere thanks to the following people, without whom this book would still be a messy pile of notes and an incomplete manuscript: my home-girl Lisa, who is always pushing me to be creative; the ever-amazing Anne Bentley, who continues to inspire me with her ability to artistically capture the essence of everything I want to say; designer extraordinaire, Rose Wright, who knew exactly what I wanted but still let me peek over her shoulder; and finally, editor-to-the-stars, Kim Carpenter, who catches all my silly mistakes in the most loving way possible. I also want to recognize the major role that the following people have had on the successful completion of this book and my life as a whole: Morgan Kertel, my muse forever; Kyle McCormick, basically the best person to ever exist (second only to Morgan); Matt McGuinness, for continuously helping to keep me alive (among other wonderful things); Chris Boral, the only second mother that I will ever need; Cheryl Duncan, my firm foundation and the most supportive human on the planet; Sydney Boral, for making me feel like I can do stuff; and finally, Hazel and Wyatt, for being the most joy-inducing furry companions to ever help write a book.

{ 95 }

On your way to the City by the Thames
(or just wish you were)?
Pick up a copy of *Local Eats London*,
also by Natasha McGuinness.